The Prince of Wales and Lord Montagu of Beaulieu in 1970 in a 12 horsepower 1899 Daimler, the car in which Lord Montagu's father, John Scott Montagu, drove the then Prince of Wales in 1899.

ROYAL CARS

James Dewar McLintock

Shire Publications Ltd

CONTENTS

Printed in Great Britain by C. I. Thomas & Sons (Haverfordwest) Ltd, Press Buildings, Merlins Bridge, Haverfordwest, Dyfed SA61 1XF.

Copyright © 1992 by James Dewar McLintock. First published 1992. Shire Album 284. ISBN 0 7478 0167 3.

British Library Cataloguing in Publication Data: McLintock, James Dewar, 1914 —. Royal cars. I. Title. 629.22220941.

Editorial Consultant: Michael E. Ware, Curator of the National Motor Museum, Beaulieu, Hampshire.

ACKNOWLEDGEMENTS
The author and publishers are grateful for the generous assistance of Chris Gill, Photographic Librarian at the National Motor Museum, Beaulieu, and Peter W. Card in the preparation of this book. The cover photograph is reproduced by kind permission of Rolls-Royce Motor Cars Limited. The other photographs are from the collection of the National Motor Museum, reproduced by kind permission, with the following exceptions: page 24 (top), acknowledged to the Tank Museum, Bovington Camp; pages 30 (top) and 31 (both), acknowledged to the Tim Graham Picture Library; and page 27 (top), acknowledged to Andrew M. Pastouna.

Cover: *The Rolls-Royce Phantom VI delivered to Her Majesty Queen Elizabeth II in 1987.*

Below: *HM The Queen with Lord Montagu in the Daimler Mail Phaeton delivered to the Prince of Wales (later Edward VII) in 1900. It was restored by the National Motor Museum in 1978 as a late Silver Jubilee present for Her Majesty.*

In 1899 at Highcliffe, Dorset, John Scott Montagu took the Prince of Wales for a drive in his 12 horsepower 1899 Daimler, an excursion which perhaps prompted the Prince to buy a Daimler of his own the following year.

THE EARLY YEARS, 1896–1918

There is no record of Queen Victoria ever having possessed a horseless carriage or ever having been driven in one. Indeed it has been said that part of the blame for the slow development of a motor industry in Britain was lack of interest at the top at a time when other European royal families sensed the potential importance of motor vehicles and were beginning to buy motor cars not just because they were novelties. But the British industry was also inhibited by hostile road regulations which had culminated in a speed restriction of 4 mph (6.4 km/h) with a man walking 20 yards (18 metres) ahead of the vehicle. The Emancipation Act of 1896 (celebrated every year in the Brighton Run) raised the speed limit to 12 mph (19 km/h), eliminated the man walking ahead and encouraged prospective investors and manufacturers. It also coincided with the awakening of the interest of the Prince of Wales (later Edward VII).

It is still not entirely clear whether Edward first drove in a car in 1896 at an Exhibition of Motors at the Imperial Institute, Kensington, London, or in 1898 at Warwick Castle or in 1899 at Highcliffe Castle near Christchurch, Dorset. Whichever the occasion, the car was a Daimler. The Prince made no move, however, until after the last occasion at Highcliffe, when John Scott Montagu, father of the present Lord Montagu of Beaulieu, took him out for a drive in the New Forest after lunch. Montagu's car was a 12 horsepower Daimler then manufactured in England under patents bought from the German company. After consulting his bicycling teacher (who later taught him to drive) and borrowing the Daimler for a week at Marlborough House, the Prince ordered one of his own: a twin-cylinder 6 horsepower Mail Phaeton

3

Left: *The 1901 Columbia Electric Phaeton used by Queen Alexandra around the estate at Sandringham. It is now privately owned but is normally on show at the National Motor Museum at Beaulieu, Hampshire.*

Right: *Edward VII in 1902, in a 24 horsepower Daimler more suited to his size, on his first motor outing after he became King.*

with a body built by Hoopers of London. It was delivered in June 1900 and was followed later in the year by two 12 horsepower models.

By 1902 (when he had become Edward VII) he had four Daimlers, including a fourteen-seater estate car, and would seem to have become an enthusiast. This was of greater importance than might now appear, for in Britain many people disapproved of motor vehicles. Royal interest was an important factor in persuading people to accept the presence on the roads of the newfangled and noisy machines which frightened the horses. *The Motor Car Journal* seemed to sum it up: 'The position which the Prince occupies at the head of British Society and the esteem in which he is held on the Continent, make his adhesion to the ranks of automobilists an event of the greatest importance, and should give an impetus not only to the industry, but also to the popularity of the motorcar as a pastime and

sport. Whilst his accession cannot fail to have its effect on the automobile movement throughout Europe, its influence in the United Kingdom will of course be more immediately felt and society people generally will naturally be less inclined to look askance at the supersession of the horse by mechanical power.' Although the King fully realised his influence, and also the importance of the home industry, he later bought three Mercedes and, for Queen Alexandra, a delightful little American-built Columbia Electric Phaeton in 1901 and a Renault landaulette. Daimlers became the official royal state cars, however — he bought several others — and remained so for the following fifty years.

One of the most notable early enthusiasts was C. S. Rolls and it was with him that the Duchess of York (later Queen Mary) took her first drive in a motor car, his Panhard of about 1899: like most other motorists, he drove a car imported from the continent. In

4

John Scott Montagu at the wheel of a 1904 22 horsepower Daimler, driving Edward VII.

Edward VII about to enter yet another royal Daimler at Dartmouth Naval College, Devon, in 1904. By 1905 he had seven Daimlers. This was one of the lighter models, which had a brisk performance.

A postcard recording what appears to be Edward VII taking an unofficial drive through Brentford, Middlesex, in the early years of his reign. The photograph is 'by Wakefield, Automobile Photographer, Brentford'.

The Duchess of York (later Queen Mary) seated beside the Honourable C. S. Rolls for her first drive in a motor car at the Hendre in 1900. The car is a c.1899 Panhard. Behind are Rolls's mother, Lady Llangattock, and Lady Eva Dugdale. The car sales and repair firm Rolls formed in 1902 specialised in selling prestigious foreign cars.

The first Rolls-Royce appeared in 1904 and this photograph is captioned 'HRH the Duke of Connaught, with Mr C. S. Rolls, in an early Rolls-Royce car'. Rolls was a captain in the recently formed Motor Volunteer Corps, members of which made themselves and their cars available for military service when required.

1902 Rolls formed his own motor agency, C. S. Rolls and Company, to import and sell prestigious foreign cars because there were still few British ones. In 1904 he met Henry Royce and began to sell Royce cars (renamed, cheekily but wisely, Rolls-Royce) and formed with Royce the famous company in 1906. Whether the Duke of Connaught owned the car in the illustration alongside is not clear but it demonstrates how quickly Rolls-Royce established a position in the market. At the beginning of the century Napier (also patronised by the Duke of Connaught) had the highest reputation as a car manufacturer in Britain but was displaced by Rolls-Royce. In common with similar companies, both Rolls-Royce and Napier ran training schools to train coachmen to be chauffeurs and mechanics.

The Duke of Connaught, the third son of Queen Victoria, in a 1902 9 horsepower two-cylinder Napier, another expensive make.

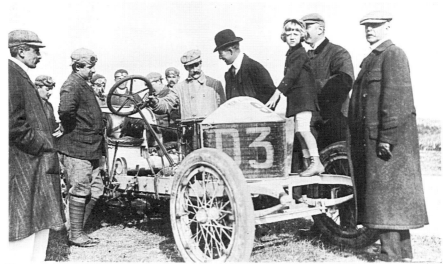

The gentleman 'au chapeau melon' (in the bowler hat) is King Albert of the Belgians and the boy clambering on the chassis is the future King Leopold. The Grand Prix racing car is thought to be a Darracq and the date is 1905.

Nicholas II, Tsar of all the Russias, on military exercises, probably in 1905. With him are the Empress and Prince Orlov. The big tourer is a French Delaunay-Belleville, one of the more costly cars of the era.

It is said that one of the most profound changes in the style of seating in motor cars was influenced by a close lady friend of King Leopold III of the Belgians. Cars were still basically modelled on horse-drawn carriages, many of which were entered from the back. When discussing with the king how his new car should be designed, she pushed a small sofa and two armchairs together, indicated where the doors should be and in effect designed the seating plan of the modern car.

King Leopold and his successor and the kings of Norway and Sweden all used Belgian Minervas, which were similar to, but livelier than Daimlers, as state cars. Young King Alfonso XIII of Spain had a very early one, too, but he was a true enthusiast and had several foreign cars. He drove a great deal, often very fast, and his passion for motoring boosted production of Hispano-Suizas, one of which was named the 'Alfonso'. Naturally he had a Benz: the first European car was popular with most

A c.1909 28 horsepower Minerva.

A baroque radiator with royal crest conceals the identity of this car, but it may be a Mercedes. There can be little doubt about the driver — King Alfonso XIII of Spain.

This Swedish state car carrying King Gustav V is a Benz of c.1908 vintage, and it is generously festooned with coronets on the headlamps, radiator cap and radiator.

Prince Wilhelm of Sweden in a huge Benz which he used for less formal royal motoring in the early 1910s. The occupants' clothing and the rear-wheel snow chains suggest Nordic temperatures.

Prince Heinrich of Prussia, brother of Kaiser Wilhelm II, here seen driving a 1911 Benz, was a motor-car enthusiast of more than ordinary technical knowledge and competed in many early reliability trials and races. The Prinz Heinrich Trials of 1908-10 were named after him.

European royal families besides the German one.

Touring at home and, for the wealthy, abroad became more common. From 1908 there was sufficient interest for Prince Heinrich of Prussia, brother of Kaiser Wilhelm II, to organise competitive touring events. As cars were modified to meet the special needs of these events the true sports car began to emerge. The first British car to be advertised as a sports car was the 3 litre Prince Henry Vauxhall (1913) designed by Laurence Pomeroy, and a notable winner of the Prinz Heinrich trials in 1910 was the 5.7 litre Prinz Heinrich Austro-Daimler designed and driven by young Ferdinand Porsche.

Many cars at the top of the market, and all state cars, were custom-built by established coachbuilders such as Barker, Hooper, Park Ward or Mulliner, who applied the same skills, techniques and, to begin with, materials as had been used for horse-drawn carriages. Perhaps the most

Prince Max of Baden (left), grandfather of the present Margrave of the state of Badenia, with his prestigious new Benz grand tourer, in the early years of the twentieth century.

11

A 1915 Daimler specially built for an Indian prince.
A 1922 40 horsepower Lanchester built for the Maharajah of Alwar.

extravagant and delightful exploitation of coachbuilding expertise, old and new, was made by overseas buyers, such as Indian rulers. It was as well that some of these cars were not driven very far as although European roads were poor they were very much better than those elsewhere. Said to be the most expensive cars, and certainly very impressive, were the French Delaunay-Bellevilles favoured by Tsar Nicholas II of Russia. They were robust vehicles, as might have been expected from a company mainly noted for producing railway locomotives and ships' boilers, and they coped well with the long distances to be travelled over slushy, muddy, poorly made Russian roads.

There is some doubt as to whether King George V (succeeded 1910) was as enthusiastic as his father about cars. During 1912 there were two new Daimlers in the garage — an extension of the mews — one being a Hooper-bodied estate car on a 57 horsepower chassis and the other a seven-seater limousine with patent leather-covered mudguards and the established dark-blue hide upholstery. Royal claret had already been accepted as the traditional exterior finish. fittings were in highly polished brass. When the King and Queen went to Sandringham or Balmoral, the cars were usually sent by rail.

Whether or not George V preferred horses to cars, he was sufficiently aware of

Above: *The Prince of Wales (later George V) with his shooting brake in 1909. The chassis is Daimler. The dog looks very comfortable.*

Above: *George V's 1911 57 horsepower six-cylinder Daimler. Note the spare wheel (one of two), even though the tyres were reliable Palmer Cords of 7 inch (18 cm) section.*

Right: *Another Daimler of the same period (1911-12) but with an undivided rear side window. The Royal Standard is being flown. Apparently Queen Mary often sat forward so that people could see her more clearly. A spare tyre is out of the way on the roof.*

13

Nagpur, India, 1912: King George V and Queen Mary in a Siddeley-Deasy — a rare marque which subsequently became the Armstrong Siddeley, with the celebrated coal-scuttle bonnet.

the importance of the burgeoning motor industry to visit Britain's new benzole production plant in 1913 and to support the campaign for home-produced fuel, which proved sufficient to render the country independent of outside sources in the years of the imminent world war. In the early days of the slump of 1931 he realised the serious effects on the motor industry and ordered five new Daimlers in order to keep more men employed.

In 1913 the King replied to a reporter that he never drove in public, although he knew how to drive and sometimes tried out cars on the estates at Sandringham and Balmoral. The royal biographer David S. Duff once said that when the King had been Prince of Wales he had liked to drive round Sandring-

Seated in the rear of this Mercedes is Kaiser Wilhelm II, and addressing him is his foreign minister. The year is 1913. This powerful car was fitted with a Knight sleeve-valve engine.

14

ham faster than Edward VII.

Nowadays a Daimler may seem a rather staid choice for a dashing student with a hectic social life but the Prince of Wales (later Edward VIII, afterwards Duke of Windsor) probably read the parental psychology well when he asked for one in 1913. It was, in any case, a smart 38 horse-power touring model. He was up at Oxford (where students were not allowed to keep cars and he had to ride a bicycle to lectures) so when his new car arrived it was put into the care of William Morris (later Lord Nuffield) at the Morris garage at Cowley. It was the last Daimler he owned until he became King in 1936 and inherited his father's cars. In between he bought a Rolls-Royce (see over), a Bentley and Hillmans. The famous black Canadian Buick DA-90, which he acquired in 1936, carried Mrs Simpson into exile in the south of France during the abdication crisis in December of that year.

In June 1914 the Archduke Franz Ferdinand was murdered at Sarajevo and in August Britain declared war on Germany. When the King visited the front he used

The interior of George V's 1913 Daimler viewed from the passenger seat.

whatever transport could be offered by the military. Usually this meant staff cars.

At a pinch almost any car will do as a staff car and at the beginning of the war the armed services were besieged with offers of cars, most often with their drivers, who were usually their owners. The ones selected for use abroad were usually big, solidly built, reliable and consequently expensive models, although Daimlers did not

The first car owned by the driver here, the Prince of Wales, later Edward VIII, then Duke of Windsor, was a 39 horsepower touring Daimler painted blue and upholstered in blue leather, given to him by his father in 1913.

Kaiser Wilhelm II (furthest from the camera in the rear seat) reviews the German troops in the First World War. The car is a Benz. These state cars had hefty 8¹/₂ litre engines. By 1926 the firm had merged with Mercedes.

stand up well to rough conditions. Rolls-Royces were highly regarded but at a premium because the company was producing the 45/50 horsepower chassis exclusively for armoured cars. The 25 horsepower D-type Vauxhall developed from the Prince Henry sports model was commissioned for staff use in great numbers. Other models that proved to be reliable were the 12/16 Sunbeam tourer and the Crossley.

The Prince of Wales acquired his first Rolls-Royce during the war as a result of a tour of the front he made with a fellow officer. It would seem that the driver of the Rolls-Royce was killed by shrapnel while he was sitting in the parked car. As his companion could not drive, the Prince first drove the driver's body to a casualty clearing station and then continued his tour. A few weeks later the Prince had the car body sent to Derby to be fitted to his first Rolls-Royce car.

King George V with the Vauxhall staff car chosen to take him across the Flanders mud to Vimy Ridge in the First World War. It is a 25 horsepower model — one of two thousand built for the War Office between 1914 and 1918.

16

The Prince of Wales touring in Western Australia in 1920. The car is a Hudson Super Six and has the badge of Prince of Wales's feathers on the bonnet.

THE TWENTIES, THIRTIES AND FORTIES

After the war many men who had encountered motor transport for the first time in the services, and who had learned to drive and maintain vehicles, were keen to acquire their own cars. By this time, and to some extent as a result of lessons learned during the war, cars were much more reliable, mass production had begun and manufacturers were quick to realise the potential for selling a much wider range of models. In spite of postwar shortages the choice in the early 1920s was very wide indeed at both the cheap and the expensive ends of the trade.

Queen Mary, who was fond of horsed carriages for official occasions, nevertheless enjoyed motoring although she is never known to have driven a car. If she was on an official visit she liked to see and be seen,

and her state car had a special high seat. She always sat bolt upright and well forward. A delightful photograph shows her being bounced about in a Citroen half-track on army manoeuvres and clearly enjoying it. How much interest she had in cars is not clear for when she was asked in the 1950s what make of car her new one would be she replied: 'I cannot remember, but I know it's a brown car.'

During the Second World War Queen Mary often gave lifts to service men and women as she was driven about the country. At first, those so favoured found that their story lacked credibility when they came to tell their friends. Accordingly, Queen Mary had hundreds of small medallions made, to serve as souvenirs by which

17

Above: *During the time he lived in England, Grand Duke Michael of Russia, the country's last Tsar (for only one day), used a splendid open touring Rolls-Royce Silver Ghost.*

Above: *King George V and Queen Mary visiting Hooper and Company (Coachbuilders), c.1925. The company was established in 1805 and built many royal carriages before going on to build royal Daimlers. It also did a lot of work for Rolls-Royce. Taken over by Daimler in 1940, the firm ceased operations in 1959.*

Below: *Victoria Eugénie, Queen of Spain, with her 1931 Austin Twenty Ranelagh limousine outside Kensington Palace in the course of a visit to England.*

18

her wartime passengers could prove that the thing had actually happened.

Prince Albert, Duke of York (later George VI), is said to have ridden a motorcycle while he was at Cambridge University, where the prohibition of cars for undergraduates was the same as at Oxford. As he seems to have been a very practical and mechanically minded man, this is not unlikely. His chauffeur was a keen motorcyclist and the Duke attended a race meeting at Brooklands in 1922, where his chauffeur was competing, and presented the prizes. Perhaps unfairly, he is the first member of the family credited with knowing much about motor-car engines: his brothers the Duke of Gloucester and, particularly, the Duke of Kent were both interested in cars.

One of his earliest cars, in 1925, was an Aster 3 litre sports saloon (Aster later merged with the Scottish car manufacturer Arrol-Johnston). Another was a 30 horsepower Lancia Kappa, which he sometimes drove with his chauffeur as passenger. Then, as now, members of the royal family were expected to set an example and not to drive recklessly or too fast. (The Prince of Wales was apparently taken to task by George V when *The Times* reported that he drove with 'enthusiastic speed'.) The Duke

Queen Mary clearly enjoying a trip downhill in a 1.3 litre Citroen Kegresse of 1922-3. It is a half-tracked adaptation of a civilian car and the model had recently crossed the Sahara Desert. The track was designed by the Tsar's French transport manager, Adolphe Kegresse, to be used to replace back wheels when the car would otherwise be bogged down in bad road and weather conditions.

A cheery scene in the paddock of Brooklands motor-racing track in 1932. The Duchess of York, later Queen Elizabeth the Queen Mother, is chatting with Mrs Billie Wisdom, one of the most successful women racers of the era. The Duke and Duchess visited motor races on several occasions.

19

The Duke and Duchess of York visited Edinburgh in connection with the Jubilee celebrations of George V in 1935. The Duchess is alighting from a Humber Pullman landaulette bearing the Royal Standard, although not a state car.

of York also bought Lanchesters before as well as after the company was acquired by Daimler and the cars became Daimlers with Lanchester radiators. He had great respect for Daimler engineering. In an official visit in 1930 he was persuaded to test how slowly a new Daimler could proceed in top gear to allow the public to have a good look at him and was very impressed by the operation of the fluid flywheel and preselector gearbox — an early form of automatic transmission.

Although the reigning monarch has been patron of the Royal Automobile Club since Edward VII accepted in 1903, it may be that official royal patronage of the Motor

The Duke and Duchess of York alight from a poppet-valve double six Daimler in 1935. The radiator mascot is Britannia above a globe. George V also used this mascot.

20

Africa, 1935: the Duke of Kent 'abandons car', perhaps wisely, as his driver prepares to make the Humber Pullman walk the planks. The big Humbers were more suitable than Daimlers for roughing it.

King George VI and the royal family in Edinburgh in 1937. The car is a 32 horsepower straight-eight 4¹/₂ litre Daimler.

King George VI, Queen Elizabeth and Princesses Elizabeth and Margaret Rose with their Lanchester cars in the New Forest in 1938. The mascot on these cars is a lion rampant.

Show began only in 1933 when it was opened by the Duke of Kent, who looked around with King Alfonso XIII as his companion. The Duke was a keen, even dashing, motorist, who was a frequent visitor to Brooklands and was president in chief of the British Racing Drivers Club. He seems to have transmitted this interest to his family for his elder son, the present Duke, was one of the first owners of an E-type Jaguar, and his other son, Prince Michael, is an Aston Martin aficionado.

In British eyes serious motor-racing is rather too dangerous for royalty but members of other royal families have competed in world-class events. Prince Nicholas of

Clearly enjoying the ride and the occasion, King George VI is taken for a drive round the Daimler works in March 1938. The car is King Edward VII's first Daimler of 1900 and the driver, George Street, had driven Edward VIII on many occasions. The car looks quite different from the restored car shown on page 2. In about 1908 the radiator was moved from under the rear body to a position at the front and a longer bonnet fabricated. At that time the car had passed through several hands and was owned by J. F. Bone.

Notable among royal princes in being a Grand Prix driver of champion class, Prince Birabongse of Siam (now Thailand) here receives the winner's cup at the first Grand Prix on the Crystal Palace circuit in London in 1937. Standing behind in the check cap is Prince Chula.

Prince Bertil of Sweden was a well informed sporting motor-car enthusiast and is here pictured in a 38/44 horsepower Bugatti roadster of the 1920s.

Rumania drove a Duesenberg at Le Mans in 1935, for example, but the most dedicated and best known royal racing driver was B. Bira — Prince Birabongse of Siam. With his cousin Prince Chula Chakrabongse he ran a number of British ERA racing cars. He won the first London Grand Prix in 1937.

As mentioned already, Daimler retained the royal warrant despite their old-fashioned styling and the introduction by Rolls-Royce in 1935 of the splendid Phantom III. Luxury cars were still most often custom-built, not only for royal use. The interior fittings were of the highest standard and included luxuries which did not become standard until more than thirty years later, such as interior lighting, effective heating and radios. The cars built for George VI were of traditionally restrained design. After he

became King in December 1936, following the abdication of Edward VIII, a new Daimler was delivered in April 1937. It was equipped not only as a state limousine, but also almost as a mobile office with its writing table, reading lamps et cetera.

The shadow of approaching war loomed over the last years of the 1930s. When there seemed to be a real threat of a German invasion a few fully armoured Humbers were constructed for the use of the royal family. They were luxuriously fitted out but this can have been small compensation for the enclosed tank-like interior. Whatever they felt about driving in these cars, the King and Queen also knew that it was important for people to see them about in wartime. Conventional Humber Pullman cars, with built-in but unobtrusive

A photograph taken in the early years of the Second World War of Queen Elizabeth alighting from the armoured Humber Special Ironside.

protection, were used instead. Royal visits to distressed, bomb-damaged areas raised morale a great deal during the war and endeared the royal family to the nation as a whole. Princess Elizabeth joined the Auxiliary Territorial Service for a brief spell, as a junior officer. Second Subaltern Elizabeth Alexandra Mary Windsor, aged eighteen, entered the ATS Mechanical Transport Training Centre near Aldershot and learned how to drive and maintain cars and other Army vehicles.

The engagement and then the marriage in 1947 of Princess Elizabeth to Prince Philip of Greece, who became Duke of Edinburgh, provided the newspapers with cheerful news at a time when it was very welcome. During their courtship he was stationed at Corsham in Wiltshire and made such good time to Buckingham Palace in his MG Midget that the Queen was worried he would have a serious accident. As it was, the smart black MG, upholstered in green, identified the visitor for whomever was watching and encouraged national speculation.

Left: *Princess Elizabeth took a Junior Officer's course with the ATS during the Second World War. It included Motor Transport Training.*

Right: *The Duke of Edinburgh congratulates H. L. Daniell, who won the 1949 Senior Tourist Trophy Race on a Norton.*

HM The Queen and the Duke of Edinburgh in a c.1952 open straight-eight Hooper-bodied Daimler on the 1954 royal tour of Australia.

QUEEN ELIZABETH II AND HER FAMILY

After his marriage the Duke of Edinburgh had a wide range of motor vehicles to choose from. Not only could he ride in, and occasionally drive, one or other of the official cars and the specialist vehicles on the estates, but he could purchase a sporty but respectable car of his own, whilst the Royal Mews was not infrequently offered 'test cars' by motor manufacturers.

Prince Philip, a past President of the Automobile Association, has a considerable respect for quality cars and over the years has driven classics such as Alvis, Lagonda, Aston Martin, Bentley and Jaguar, the latter including the legendary D-type sports-racer. He drove a record-breaking Rover gas-turbine car at the factory and for a couple of years owned a remarkable prototype called the Reliant-Triplex GTS, built by Ogle Design of Letchworth. He first saw it at the 1965 Motor Show, subsequently acquired it and perhaps unwittingly enhanced the reputation of its creators. The production version became the Reliant Scimitar GTE, an example of which was owned by Princess Anne.

It has been said that the Duke of Edinburgh was responsible for the adoption of

The Jaguar Mark VII/IX acquired in 1955 by Queen Elizabeth the Queen Mother.

The Duke of Kent with his third car, an Aston Martin coupé, DB2/4, 1955, with a 3 litre twin-camshaft engine of Lagonda (W. O. Bentley) design.

Rolls-Royces as state cars. In 1948 the firm had an experimental model nicknamed the 'Scalded Cat' on account of the performance conferred by its $5^1/2$ litre straight-eight engine. Prince Philip had it on loan for a week and was so impressed that a production version — the first Phantom IV — was ordered for Princess Elizabeth in July 1950. Only eighteen were ever built. A more likely reason for the change is that Daimler stopped making the long-wheelbase models while the Rolls-Royce Phantom IV not only had a 12 foot (3.7 metre) wheelbase but gave superior performance.

The Duke of Edinburgh was very interested in this experimental 1965 Reliant-Triplex GTS plastic-bodied coupé and used it extensively.

26

HM The Queen with the Governor of the State of Mysore being driven through Bangalore in 1961 in an open Daimler straight-eight.

HM The Queen and the Duke of Edinburgh in the Rolls-Royce Phantom V delivered in 1961. The perspex rear section can be covered by an aluminium two-piece hood.

Top: *A Rolls-Royce Phantom V State Landaulette of 1964.*

Above: *The Rolls-Royce Phantom VI (1978) given to HM The Queen as a Jubilee gift by the Society of Motor Manufacturers and Traders.*

Below left: *Interior of the Rolls-Royce Phantom V State Landaulette shown at the top of the page.*

Below right: *Interior of the Rolls-Royce Phantom VI shown above.*

While Daimler lost the prestige of supplying the state cars, for after that time Rolls-Royce always supplied them, Daimler have never been far away from the royal household, because Jaguar bought Daimler in 1960 and put Daimler grilles on Jaguars. Moreover, Queen Elizabeth the Queen Mother has a 1990 Daimler limousine and Her Majesty The Queen acquired a new one in April 1992.

In 1992 the most recent state car is the 1987 Phantom VI, whilst an earlier Phantom VI is the one which was presented to the Queen by the British motor industry in 1978. There are two Phantom V models of 1960 and 1961 vintage and a Phantom IV which dates back to 1948 and has 150,000 miles (240,000 km) or more to its credit.

Other cars at the Palace include the two Daimler limousines, two Ford Granada estates, a Range-Rover, a Rover minibus and a Land-Rover. The cars have been converted to run on unleaded petrol, but 'greenest' of all is the Bedford electric runabout which Prince Philip uses occasionally to make short trips in London.

The Prince and Princess of Wales have a Bentley and a Jaguar V12 for official duties. The Bentley is usually chauffeur-driven but the Jaguar is for less formal use and is from time to time driven by both Charles and Diana. The Prince has a wide

The beautiful scale model of a Grand Prix racing Sunbeam presented to the young Lord Nicholas Windsor, son of the Duke of Kent, by the trustees of the National Motor Museum in 1972.

choice, since he has two classics — a 1971 DB6 Mk 2 Aston Martin Volante and a 1987 V8 Volante. The earlier car was a 21st birthday present from Her Majesty The Queen. In 1992 the Princess controversially acquired a Mercedes 500SL.

The Duke of Gloucester became a member of the Institute of Advanced Motorists in 1965. Some years later he took a high-performance course and around this time

Prince Charles and Earl Mountbatten of Burma with Lord Montagu at the National Motor Museum, Beaulieu, in 1974, looking at the Columbia Electric Phaeton illustrated on page 4.

29

The Prince of Wales in his Aston Martin at Clarence House visiting Queen Elizabeth the Queen Mother on her birthday in 1986.

he was elected president of the IAM, an office he still holds. The Duke of Kent was the first member of the royal family to pass the IAM test and his brother, Prince Michael, soon followed his example. One of the earliest IAM members was The Honourable Gerald Lascelles.

Both the Duke of Gloucester and Prince Michael of Kent are accomplished riders of superbikes when opportunity arises. The Duke of Kent is an honorary member of the Guild of Motoring Writers and President of the Automobile Association. In 1972 he opened the National Motor Museum at Beaulieu, of which Prince Michael is a trustee. Prince Michael has an Aston Martin but is also fond of his Ford Cosworth Sierra and drives a great deal. In 1988 the Prince was co-driver with Lord Montagu when they drove a 1914 Rolls-Royce in the Australian Castrol World Rally over a 2500 mile (4000 km) route including the awesome Nullarbor desert. The Prince regularly takes part in the London-Brighton run.

Prince Michael of Kent driving a 1956 Aston Martin DBR2 in the 1988 Mille Miglia.

The Princess of Wales driving her Ford Sierra Cosworth in 1988.

The Duke of Edinburgh in 1991 on a visit to the Innovation Centre, London Docklands, in his Bedford Electric runabout.

FURTHER READING

McLintock, J. Dewar. *Royal Motoring*. G. T. Foulis, 1962.
Montagu of Beaulieu, Lord. *Royalty on the Road*. Collins, 1980.
Pastouna, Andrew M. *The Royal Rolls-Royce Motor Car*. Osprey, 1991.
Smith, Brian E. *Royal Daimlers*. Transport Book Publications, 1976.

PLACES TO VISIT

Museum displays may be altered and readers are advised to telephone before visiting to check that relevant items are on show, as well as to find out the opening times.

Museum of British Road Transport, St Agnes Lane, Hales Street, Coventry, West Midlands CV1 1PN. Telephone: 0203 832425.
National Motor Museum, John Montagu Building, Beaulieu, Brockenhurst, Hampshire SO42 7ZN. Telephone: 0590 612345.
Sandringham Museum, Sandringham House, King's Lynn, Norfolk PE35 6EN. Telephone: 0553 772675.

HM The Queen with Lord Montagu inspecting the restored 1900 Daimler Mail Phaeton which had belonged to her great-grandfather.